THE POWER OF
FAITH
CAN MOVE
MOUNTAINS

Rev J Martin

DEDICATION

I dedicate this book to my family, for their constant love and support.

CONTENTS

ACKNOWLEDGMENTS

This book would not have been possible without the support and encouragement of my family, and the inspiration from my Heavenly Father.

A special thanks to: my editor; Pixal Design Studios for the design work, and Amazon for providing the digital tools by which I can get my message out into the world.

Finally, I would like to thank YOU, for buying my book, may it enlighten your life and bring you peace.

Introduction

In life, we all face mountains, difficulties that can seem insurmountable. Your doctor might have told you that you will never get well. Your relationship could be on the rocks, and you don't know how you will stay together. It could be a mountain in your financial life; it doesn't look like you will ever get out of debt or ever accomplish your dreams.

Many people pray about their mountains. They will describe them and inform God of the exact dimensions of the mountain, reporting to Him what a hindrance it is in their life. They might even use the problem as an excuse for non-action.

Many people will pray, asking God to speak to their mountain. God, please help me to overcome my sickness. God help beat this addiction. God, please help my brother to turn his life around.

Yes, it is good to pray; it is good to ask God for help. But when you face a mountain, it not enough to pray. It's not enough to believe and think good thoughts.

Mark 11:23

"Truly I tell you, if anyone says to this mountain, 'Go, throw yourself into the sea,' and does not doubt in their heart but believes that what they say will happen, it will be done for them."

As Jesus said, you must speak to your mountain. He didn't say pray to your mountain; you need to say, "Problem be gone. I will not allow you in my life."

Combined with praying, you need to talk to that sickness. Sickness, you have no right in my body; I am not asking you to leave. I'm commanding you to leave. This is the faith Jesus was talking about.

What most people do is label the sickness; they call it by name, my sore leg, my sore back. They give it an identity; therefore, it grows in their lives. Like an unwanted guest in your house, let it know it is not welcome.

Back Chat

If you don't speak to your mountains, your mountains will talk to you. Throughout the day, the negative thoughts will say, the pain will never go away; you'll never get a better job; you can forget all about fulfilling your dreams.

Now, you can sit back and believe the negative thoughts and be overcome with feelings of worry, doubt, and fear, or you can rise up in faith and say, wait a minute – I am in control here, and I will achieve great things.

You may be dealing with a situation that looks like it will never change; it might look like you will never overcome your fears; it may look like you will never lose weight or never achieve your dreams. Fear will tell you your problems are insurmountable.

Praying and believing are good, but if you will see your problems move, you need to speak to them. Say, sickness you have to go, debt you are no longer welcome in my life, depression you will not steal my destiny.

When you speak words of faith to your mountain daily and do not doubt, it allows divine power to flow into your life, and your mountain will be removed.

Now it may not happen overnight. You may speak to the mountain, and it will look the same from one day to the next, don't worry about it. God works at a slower pace than we do, but be assured, once you ask, you will receive.

Hebrews 11:6
And without faith it is impossible to please God.

First Steps

In mid-December, I had an accident and severely fractured my fifth metatarsal, meaning, I had to wear a cast boot for 12 weeks. At the start of March, I got the all-clear, but the doctor said the bone I had damaged was one of the slowest healing bones in the body and could take up to 6 months to heal.

I still had a slight pain annoying me, but from my doctor's advice, I decided not to push myself too much until it went away.

Being housebound for so long, I didn't get to make my regular visits to a friend. Noel had a terrible break-up involving three children, which resulted in him being very angry and having a very negative view on life.

Rather than being overjoyed to see me, he was furious; he felt I had left him stranded, without an outlet. Rather than being concerned about me, he kept referring to how bad his life had been without my visits.

Always thinking of others and not myself, I visited him, but he constantly reminded me I had let him down, never once asking how I was.

One day, when I was speaking words of faith over my foot, God talked to me in the form of a thought, "For your faith to work, you will need to keep negative people out of your life."

So, I slowly distanced myself from him, and daily, I spoke to my bone saying, 'I am healed and at full strength.' Within a month, the pain was gone.

I share this story with you, because negative people and those of little faith affect the power of your faith. It works on so many levels; often, we can share our wisdom with others who automatically shoot us down, which can instill doubt in our minds.

For your faith to move the mountains in your life, your faith must be at its highest level, which means you must remove or distance yourself from those who are negative or fill you with doubt.

Apple A Day

As I had limited movement for over three months, when I got back on my feet, I was surprised how unfit I had become. Without daily exercise, I was overweight, and my muscles were frail.

They say everything happens for a reason, and I believe my accident happened for me to appreciate how much fitness affects a person's state of mind. It made me realize some people don't have strong faith because they don't feel well.

One of the most important things you can do is to go to work on your health; a lot of things come from that. The power of your faith can be greatly diminished by being lazy.

Most illnesses come from not looking after yourself, both mentally and physically. Some people, after abusing their bodies for years, want a miracle cure; unless you treat the core of the problem, eating healthy and exercising regularly, even a miracle will be short-lived.

If you take care of yourself, looking at your health as a support system for the body and mind, you cannot believe what is possible. You cannot believe the power of your faith when you have the health and energy to say; I will go to work on this problem; I feel healthy, I feel vigorous, and I'm not out of breath.

Sometimes, when difficulties come and you're weak, you will say, I don't think I can do that; that mountain is too big; please God, help me to live with this mighty mountain.

Doubts in life are often more physical than mental. You haven't got the vitality to believe it is possible, but if you have the strength and you've got the health, I'm telling you the power of your faith will shock you.

Congregation Moves Mountain

The following story is taken from reported events.

A small congregation in the foothills of the Great Smokies built a new sanctuary on a piece of land given to them by a church member. Ten days before the new church was to open, the local building inspector informed the pastor that the parking lot was inadequate for the size of the building.

Until the church doubled the size of the parking lot, they could not use the new sanctuary. Unfortunately, the church had used every inch of their land, except for the mountain against which it had been built. To create more parking spaces, they would have to move the mountain out of the back yard.

Undeterred, the pastor announced the next Sunday morning he would meet that evening with all members who had "mountain moving faith." They would hold a prayer session, asking God to remove the mountain from the back yard and to provide enough money, somehow, to have it paved and painted before the scheduled opening dedication service the following week.

At the appointed time, 24 of the congregation's 300 members assembled for prayer. They prayed for nearly three hours. At ten o'clock, the pastor said the final "Amen." "We'll open next Sunday as scheduled," he assured everyone. "God has never let us down before, and I believe He will be faithful this time too."

The next morning, as the pastor was working in his study, there came a loud knock at his door. When he called "come in," a rough looking construction foreman appeared, removing his hard hat as he entered.

"Excuse me, Reverend. I'm from Acme Construction Company over in the next county. We're building a huge new shopping mall over there, and we need some landfill. Would you be willing to sell us a chunk of that mountain behind the church? We'll pay you for what we remove and pave all the exposed area free of charge if we can have it right away. We can't do anything until we get the landfill and allow it to settle."

The little church opened the next Sunday as originally planned, and there were far more members in attendance with "mountain moving faith" than there had been the previous week!

If you will see your mountains move, you need to speak to your mountains. Often, we do the exact opposite; we talk about the mountain to anyone that will listen.

Talking about our problems makes them bigger. "I just don't see how I'm ever going to overcome this issue; me change, at my age? It's better if I just stay where I am. In time, I will get used to it."

When you talk negatively like this, you magnify the problem, making it bigger, making it worse.

When faced with a challenge, this is how most people deal with it. They talk about their problems, not realizing this approach just makes them bigger.

We all face difficulties in life, but when the negative thoughts come telling you how bad it is, how you're never going to make it, never be healthy, never be happy, learn to turn them around.

Say to the mountain of doubt, mountain of worry, mountain of fear. You will not keep me from my destiny; you will not dominate my thought life. God has promised I will achieve great things. So, I am not asking you to leave; I'm commanding you to leave.

This is the faith that can move mountains.

Deuteronomy 30:9
The LORD will again delight in you and make you prosperous, just as He delighted in your ancestors.

Mark 11

One spring afternoon, Jesus and His disciples were walking across the dry Middle East desert, when they came upon a lonesome fig tree. When they approached it, they found nothing but leaves. Then, Jesus said to the fig tree, "May no one ever eat fruit from you again."

The next day, on their journey back, Peter saw the fig tree had withered from the roots. "Rabbi!" he said. "The fig tree you cursed has withered!"

With that miracle, Jesus spoke on the subject of faith. "Have faith in God," Jesus answered. " Truly I tell you, if anyone says to this mountain, `Go, throw yourself into the sea,' and does not doubt in their heart but believes that what he says will happen, it will be done for him."

Jesus did not pray about the fig tree; he didn't say I believe the fig tree will not produce any fruit. I'm hoping it will not produce fruit. No, He commanded it not to produce fruit.

Command your sickness to leave your body; you have to command depression to get out of your life. Command division to get out of your family.

If you say to your mountain, be removed, you will have what you say; your mountain responds to your voice. I can speak faith over you all day long; friends can build you up with words of encouragement, all of which is important, but your mountain is not interested in what other people are saying. It is only interested in what you are saying. It only responds to your voice.

When you rise up in faith and say, sickness, addiction, depression, in the name of Jesus you have to go, that's when the forces of heaven come to attention.

Faith is the most powerful force God has given us. With it, we can receive remarkable results and experience the impossible. "Nothing is impossible to those that believe."

The Mountain Climber

There was a mountain climber whose lifelong dream was to conquer the Aconcagua in the Andes. After years of preparation, he started the climb alone, as he wanted the glory to himself.

As he climbed, all his training had paid off. Within hours, he was well beyond his planned camping spot. Believing he could make it to the top before nightfall, he kept going.

Darkness fell quicker than expected and clouds covered the night sky; making visibility almost zero. As he moved towards one of the last ridges, he slipped and fell. Falling rapidly, he reached out to grab something but only found empty air. He kept falling; in them last few moments life flashed through his mind. He was certain he would die.

But then, he felt a jolt that almost tore him in half; the rope that he had staked caught the last pin. Suspended in the air, not knowing if the last pin would hold, he shouted into the heavens,

"Please God, help me!" There was nothing but silence, so he shouted again. "Help me, please, help me!" Then, there was a deep voice that seemed to echo up the mountain…. " What do you want me to do?"

"Please save me."

"Do you really think I can save you?" God asked.

"Of course, just tell me what to do."

"Ok, just cut the rope that is holding you up."

There was another moment of silence. The man just held tighter to the rope. The rescue team says, the next day, they found a frozen mountain climber hanging firmly to a rope...

Two feet off the ground.

Like this mountain climber, its often when we are closest to victory that we get our ultimate test. Anyone can have strong faith when things are going good; it's when problems arise that our character develops.

James 1:6
But when you ask, you must believe and not doubt, because the one who doubts is like a wave of the sea, blown and tossed by the wind.

Healing Touch

In the scripture, there was a paralyzed man. One day, he heard Jesus was in town and would preach at a nearby house. The man convinced four of his friends to carry him to where Jesus would be.

When they got there, they were too late; the place was already packed. It was so crowded they couldn't get in. He could have easily gotten discouraged and turned back, but the paralyzed man would not take no for an answer. He was determined. He wanted to be healed. He knew you are closest to your victory when you come up against your greatest opposition.

A man alone would have problems getting to Jesus, never mind four men carrying a stretcher; he had come up against a mountain, an insurmountable task, but not to this man. He knew that, with the right amount of faith, anything was possible.

Many people, when faced with adversity, give up. They get bad news from their doctor and don't even think of going for a second opinion or searching for alternative treatments. They fail to get one job, so don't apply for anymore positions, thinking they are not capable. They have a problem in their relationship, and rather than sit down and have a heart to heart conversation, they believe another relationship is the answer.

For me, getting through the roof is a metaphor for having a mountain in your life and not letting the circumstances stop you. I'm sure the place was packed that day; there were people in the doorway, sitting in the windows. Turning back would have been easy, but it wasn't an option for the paralyzed man.

He probably said to his friends, "I have an idea. Take me up on the roof, cut a hole in it, and lower me down, so I can be close to Jesus." Where there's a will, there is always a way.

Mark 2:5
When Jesus saw their faith, he said to the paralyzed man, "Son, your sins are forgiven."

I'm sure it wasn't easy to hoist the man up on the roof, dig the hole, and lower him down, but they did it. Seeing the man's faith, Jesus forgave him of his sins, and later, the paralyzed man walked out of the house, healed.

Many people there that day were also looking for a miracle, people a lot closer to Jesus. What was the difference? The paralyzed man's actions symbolized the level of faith He was teaching His disciples when talking about the mustard seed and throwing the mountain into the sea.

God is looking for a faith he can see, not just a faith he can hear: not just a faith that believes, but a faith that is visible, a faith demonstrated.

Two Components Of Faith

A man, who heard about faith moving mountains, said to himself, "I'm going to try this faith stuff. I want to see if it works." So, he got up early one morning and said to his overgrown back garden, "I command all the weeds to die." Nothing happened.

The next morning, upon waking he rushed down stairs and looked out his kitchen window. To his dismay, the garden was still overgrown. He exclaimed, "I knew it wouldn't work!"

This man forgot an important component of faith: BELIEF. As Jesus said, 'if anyone says, and does not doubt.' This man did not believe; he only spoke doubt filled words. True faith has two components: BELIEVING and SPEAKING.

In 2 Corinthians 4:13 we read: "It is written: `I believed; therefore I have spoken.' Since we have that same spirit of faith, we also believe and: therefore speak. Believing and speaking go together. Many people are speaking without believing, and therefore are not receiving what they desire.

Lost at Sea

When Moses was caught between the Red Sea and Pharaoh's entire cavalry, the people were terribly frightened, and cried out to the Lord to help them. Then they turned to Moses, whining, "Have you brought us out here to die in the desert because there were not enough graves for us in Egypt?"

Then in Exodus 14:15, God strangely asked Moses, "Why are you crying out to Me?" What a strange question for God to ask? You would think God would be happy His people were crying out to Him. But He wasn't!

"Tell the Israelites to move forward," was His command. Can you imagine hearing those words, while looking at the roaring Red Sea? "Move forward."

The fearful people must have thought, 'God must be joking around with us.' But at God's command, Moses stretched forth his rod to part the waters, and the people marched forward.

We can extract an important truth from this story: Sometimes, God wants us to move forward in faith, and expectancy, rather than waiting, praying, fearing the worst.

Not By What You See

2 Corinthians 5:7
For we live by faith, not by sight.

Paul was saying, don't live by what you see, keeping your eyes - your attention – on your difficulty, looking for confirmation that your words are working. Be confident your words of faith must work— they must produce.

All too often, if we don't see the situation change as quickly as we would like, we can get discouraged; fearful thoughts can begin to cloud our mind; meaning, worry and stress can consume us.

Instead of letting negative thoughts in, do what Abraham did when God appeared to him with the good news that his wife would have a baby. He changed his name from Abram to Abraham— before his wife conceived!

Abraham means "father of many nations". Can you imagine having the faith to call yourself the father of many nations, yet not having even one child to carry on your name?

Abraham was speaking to his mountain; we must follow in his footsteps, he is the founding father of faith. Don't speak about how the pain, problem, or difficulty is still there. Announce the end from the beginning. I am healthy. I am successful. I am filled with happiness and joy.

Like with Abraham changing his name, we too must change the language we use every day. Speaking words of faith, love, and joy. This is a vital step in both the recovery and the maintenance of our mental and physical health.

Almost the Power Of God

In the book of Genesis, God said let there be light and there was light; those words created light; people will say, Yeah, God's words can create light.

What I have learnt is—human words can be almost as powerful; words can create the light of insight, not the light of the sun, but the light of consciousness. Human words can do that; that is the power of speaking words of faith. Within faith, there is an unseen magic.

Just say you cannot see a way to be happy or overcome your fears, and someone comes along and tells you their story. They explain to you the power of forgiving all those that have hurt you in the past.

Then you try it for yourself, and a mountain in your life is removed, and you become happier than you have been in years. Here's what you will say; before you came into my life, I was blind; before you got here, I was living in the darkness behind a mighty mountain, but now, I can see the glorious rays of the sun.

We, as children of God, have the unique ability to change our lives and those around us with language; do not be lazy with language— with language, you can unlock a person's potential, awaken their faith, opening their eyes to something they have never seen before.

And, this experience of insight can be the turning point in their life, the beginning of a new career, a new relationship, or a life without pain. Speak faith over your life and those around you; it is so powerful.

So, I'm asking you to speak to your mountains. Use words of faith in your personal life, family life, and business life. Talk about solutions, not problems, and advise others to do the same.

Language can be the bridge that takes you from the darkness to the light, from living in fear to living in faith, from not knowing to knowing.

John 14:12
Very truly I tell you, whoever believes in me will do the works I have been doing, and they will do even greater things than these, because I am going to the Father.

Kill Your Fears

When David faced Goliath, everyone was talking about Goliath; they were saying how big he was, how strong he was, and how no man could defeat him. David was only 17, and up to this point, he was but a simple farmer.

But David understood this principle; he said, "Who is this Philistine that he should defy the armies of the living God?" David simply could not believe one man was holding back an entire army in fear.

One mountain would keep them from their destiny; he was having none of that. Everyone made fun of him, even David's brother, but he still went out to face his mountain.

Then, Goliath made fun of him. He looked David over and saw he was little more than a boy, glowing with health and handsome, and he despised him. Then he said to David, "Am I a dog, that you come at me with sticks? Come here, and I'll give your flesh to the birds and the wild animals!"

David just didn't pray that he would beat Goliath; he just didn't believe or hope he would defeat him. David spoke to his mountain. "You come against me with sword and spear, but I come against you in the name of the Lord Almighty, the God of the armies of Israel, whom you have defied. This day the Lord will deliver you into my hands, and I'll strike you down and cut off your head."

David knew, when he spoke to his mountain, it would be removed. If you will see significant changes, you need to talk to the mountains in your life.

Some of you might be facing problems you simply cannot see a way to get over or around. Your relationship could be on the rocks, debts are mounting up, and your health could be dragging you down.

You could be standing exactly where David stood, with a mountain in your path. It's not enough to pray or believe it will move out of your way. You must command it to move to one side.

Say to the mountain of worry, doubt, or fear, "You come against me with natural weapons, but I come against you in the name of the Lord. And I know with words of faith you will be removed."

Incredible energy is released when we speak to our mountains. Instead of talking to God about how big your problems are, speak to your problems about how big your God is.

The more you talk about your mountain, the weaker it will make you. Well, the doctor said my sickness might never go away. I've prayed, but my marriage isn't getting any better. I've tried to stop drinking, but I keep going back to it. Why bother?

When you talk like this, all it is doing is making you weaker, have less faith, have less energy. Stop talking about the mountain and start talking to the mountain. Like David said, I will defeat you. You need to say to that sickness, sickness you are no longer welcome in my body; with the will of God I will get rid of you.

Declare to the addiction, the power that is within me is greater than the power that's within you. You will not keep me from health; I will defeat you.

In life, we will always have mountains trying to keep us from God's best; it's good to pray, it's good to believe, but it's only when we talk to our mountains, letting them know they are no longer welcome, that action happens.

Mountain of doubt, you will not defeat me. I speak health over my body, faith over my life, and blessings into my future.

Molehill Over Mountains

In my life, I've succeeded at turning molehills into mountains. There have been situations that were no big deal, but I lost sleep over them. I've also allowed real problems to make my faith waiver.

There are times when we face insurmountable odds and impossibilities; problems can seem so big, they block our view of God. We tell ourselves we have no chance of success, so we shouldn't even bother trying.

A mountain of doubt can make our faith seem to look like level ground.

When you meet difficulties, don't complain, don't talk defeat, dig your heels in and speak favor over the situation. You might have problems in your relationship.

Don't complain about the problem; speak about the solution. It's all about perspective.

Jesus told us we need little faith to cast mountains out of our path. We don't have to have the ability; we just need the faith to believe God is able.

When you speak to your mountain, when you declare God's favor, this activates the power of the most high. That's when our mountains will turn to molehills.

Zechariah 4:7

"What are you, mighty mountain? Before Zerubbabel you will become level ground. And when he sets the final stone of the Temple in place, the people will shout: 'May God bless it! May God bless it!'"

Are there mountains holding you back that you want to become level ground? It could be a mountain in your career, or a mountain in your relationship, or a mountain of worry or guilt. Your mind will tell you the problem is permanent; that it will never change.

Your challenge is to speak to those mountains, be removed; you will not defeat me. Learn to speak favor over the situation. There is nothing stronger than speaking favor over your life.

Some of you have talked about your mountains long enough; you need to talk to your mountains. If you rise and say to the sickness, say to the worry, say to the depression, be removed; you've got to go.

Do this, and you will overcome obstacles that seem permanent. You will fulfill dreams you thought were impossible, and you will achieve all God has planned for you. Like Zerubbabel, your mighty mountain will become level ground.

Moving Begins

Does God still perform miracles, today? He does. Every time you stretch your faith, God does miracles — every single time. What's the mountain in your life that must be removed? What's the thing you've already decided will never change?

How do you know that it won't change?

Maybe God wants your faith to over ride the laws of nature. He has in the past; He is doing it all around the world today. God is in the mountain-moving business. Do not underestimate what He can do in your life.

Matthew 13:58 says, "Jesus did not do many miracles there because of their lack of faith." Are you seeing with eyes of fear, worry, or doubt, or are you seeing with eyes of faith? Faith opens the door to miracles.

Now, I know how hard it can sometimes be when health and financial problems can seem insurmountable, and often, in these times, our faith is tested. There are two steps I recommend that may not be easy but are essential to living a healthy successful life.

Act I

The essence of Jesus' teaching was to love and to forgive. The first step in any health issue is first to forgive anyone that has hurt or mistreated you. This can be a hard step for many people to take, as often the pain is due to someone's actions, which changed the direction of their life.

It is important to remember you do not forgive for their benefit or saying what they did was right; forgiving is for your benefit. In the eyes of God, you are the bigger person; your spirit will be cleansed.

An important step, which is often overlooked, is to forgive yourself. All too often, we keep going over all the mistakes we made in the past. When you ask for forgiveness, you will be forgiven. Accept the forgiveness.

Occasionally, your mistake may pop into your mind, and if it does, be thankful for the forgiveness you have already received; turn a fear thought into a thought of faith.

Act II

To succeed means sharing your gifts; we all have been graced with unique qualities given to us to make this world a better place. Not using them leads to the withering of our spirit, which can manifest itself in depression, illness, and pain.

All too often, I hear people complain about their job, how it is not rewarding. They simply are waiting for the weekend. This is not what we were created to do, wish our life away working jobs we dislike.

We all have been graced with many talents. Some of us have the gift of communication; some people are good with their hands; some people are leaders, and others like to provide service.

Many people, when asked what they would like to do with their lives, will give you a blank face of confusion. For me, it is the way the question is asked.

A better way to phrase the question is, what service would you like to provide to the world?

A few simple words of encouragement can instill faith in someone, changing the direction of their lives, so not only can you move the mountains in your own life, but also in the lives of others.

From today, use the words— I can— I will— I must. Move forward with positive expectancy and watch amazing things flow into your life.

ABOUT THE AUTHOR

I live on the northwest coast of Ireland. I use this medium to share my true voice. I wish to enlighten others and help them to see that God wants the very best for them. We often make it hard for him to enter our lives as we focus on the dark clouds rather than the silver lining.

In this growing digital frontier I just want to shed a little light out into the world to light up peoples lives in the hope that they to will help inspire others which will slowly but surely change the world, even in a small way.

My Other Books

God's Perfect Timing
The Power Of Letting Go
The Power Of Choice
The Power Of Words
Make Space for God

Made in the USA
San Bernardino, CA
27 May 2018